Fasting the Biblical Way Journal

This Book Belongs To

_____

_____

_____

Copyright © 2023. All rights reserved.

ERICA BASORA

No part of this content may be reproduced or transmitted for commercial purposes in any form or by any means, electronic or mechanical, including photocopying and recording, or by any data retrieval or storage system. information whatsoever, unless authorized in writing by the author.

Introduction

The **"The Fasting the Biblical Way Journal"** offers a haven of reflection amidst life's relentless chaos, where the noise of the world often drowns out our innermost thoughts. It serves as more than mere bound pages; it is a sanctuary for the faithful and a refuge for those seeking spiritual connection.

Within its pages, readers embark on a spiritual journey, drawing inspiration from the enduring wisdom of Daniel's fast—an embodiment of unwavering faith, steadfast prayer, and divine guidance. Here, solace and purpose are discovered as one explores the fundamental facets of their relationship with the Divine: prayer, gratitude, and the profound desires that stir within.

This journal comprises four distinct sections:

Prayer Request: A space to pour out hopes, dreams, and concerns, knowing that God hears every word.

Prayers Answered: A testament to the faithfulness of divine intervention, where answered prayers, both significant and small, are documented.

Things I am Grateful for: An opportunity to nurture a heart of thanksgiving by recognizing daily blessings.

What is on my heart: A canvas for the deepest corners of one's soul to find expression, allowing for the articulation of fears, desires, and musings in an environment that celebrates vulnerability.

This journal serves as a loyal companion, guiding individuals through the intricacies of their spiritual and emotional landscapes. Through prayer, gratitude, and the earnest expression of one's heart, it illuminates the profound joy of communion with the Divine, facilitating a transformative journey within the depths of the soul.

*Accompany this journal and provide space for reflection and worship with the Spotify playlist Fasting the Biblical Way.

Daily Devotion

Day 1

Isaiah 58:6-7

"Is not this the kind of fasting I have chosen: to loose the chains of injustice and untie the cords of the yoke, to set the oppressed free and break every yoke? Is it not to share your food with the hungry and to provide the poor wanderer with shelter— when you see the naked, to clothe them, and not to turn away from your own flesh and blood?"

Daily Devotional

Date:

M ☐ T ☐ W ☐ T ☐ F ☐ S ☐ S ☐

Verse of The Day

_____
_____
_____

Key Words	Question

Reflection

_____
_____
_____

How Will I Apply This To My Life	My Prayerful Responses

Prayer

Date: _____

For Loved Ones _____

Self _____

Todays' Prayer Focus

_____
_____
_____
_____
_____
_____

Prayer Points

_____
_____
_____
_____
_____
_____
_____
_____
_____
_____
_____

Prayer journal

Today's Date:

Today what is on my heart:

Today I am grateful for:

Prayer Request

Prayers Answered

Daily Devotion

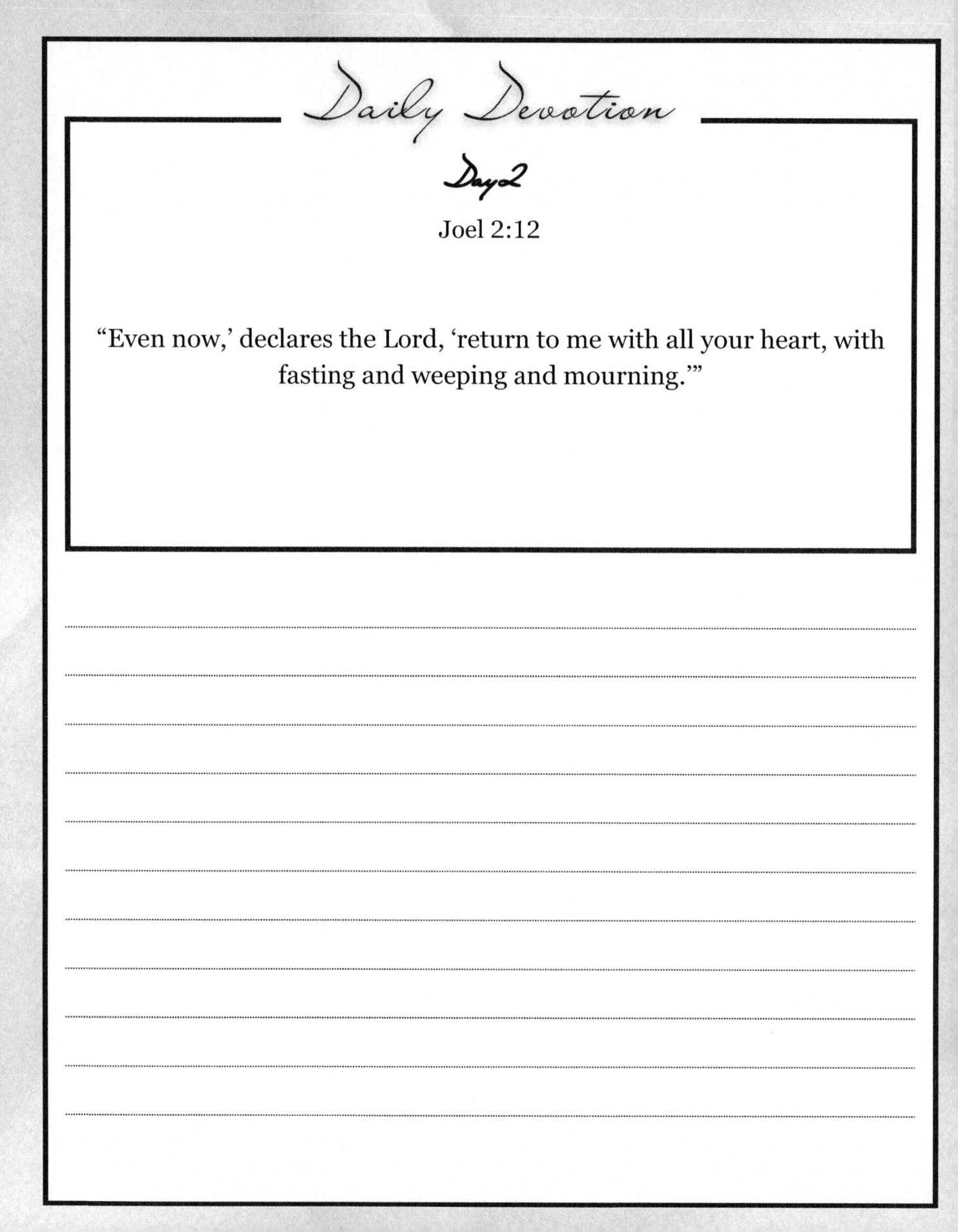

Day 2

Joel 2:12

"Even now,' declares the Lord, 'return to me with all your heart, with fasting and weeping and mourning.'"

Daily Devotional

Date:

M ☐ T ☐ W ☐ T ☐ F ☐ S ☐ S ☐

Verse of The Day

_____
_____
_____

Key Words	Question

Reflection

_____
_____
_____

How Will I Apply This To My Life	My Prayerful Responses

Date:_____

Prayer

For Loved Ones _____

Self _____

Todays' Prayer Focus

_____
_____
_____
_____
_____

Prayer Points

_____
_____
_____
_____
_____
_____
_____
_____
_____
_____

Prayer journal

Today's Date:

Today what is on my heart:

Today I am grateful for:

Prayer Request

Prayers Answered

Daily Devotion

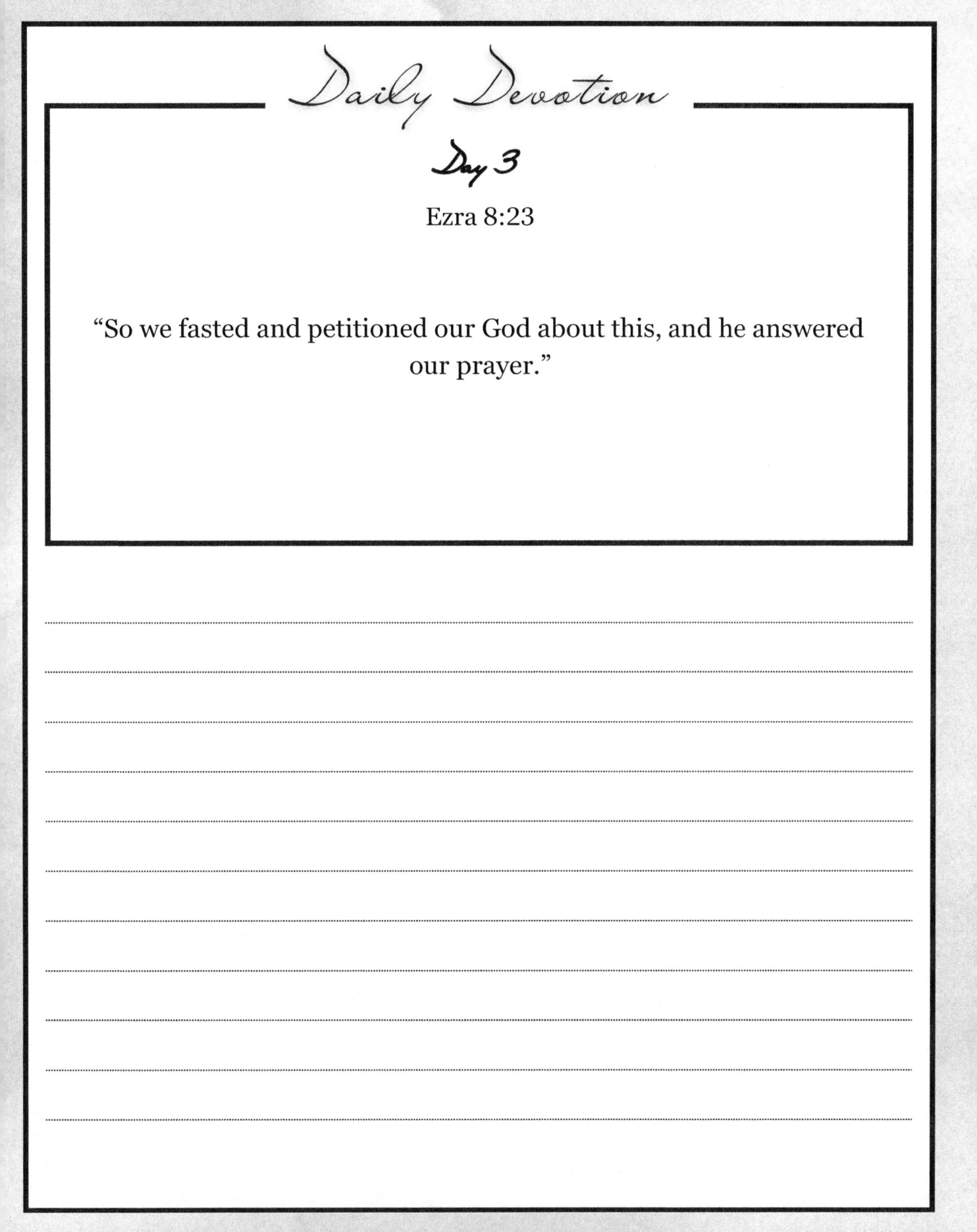

Day 3

Ezra 8:23

"So we fasted and petitioned our God about this, and he answered our prayer."

Daily Devotional

Date:

M☐ T☐ W☐ T☐ F☐ S☐ S☐

Verse of The Day

_____
_____
_____

Key Words	Question

Reflection

_____
_____
_____

How Will I Apply This To My Life	My Prayerful Responses

Prayer

Date:_____

For Loved Ones _____

Self _____

Todays' Prayer Focus

_____
_____
_____
_____
_____
_____

Prayer Points

_____
_____
_____
_____
_____
_____
_____
_____
_____
_____

Prayer journal

Today's Date:

Today what is on my heart:

Today I am grateful for:

Prayer Request

Prayers Answered

# Daily Devotion

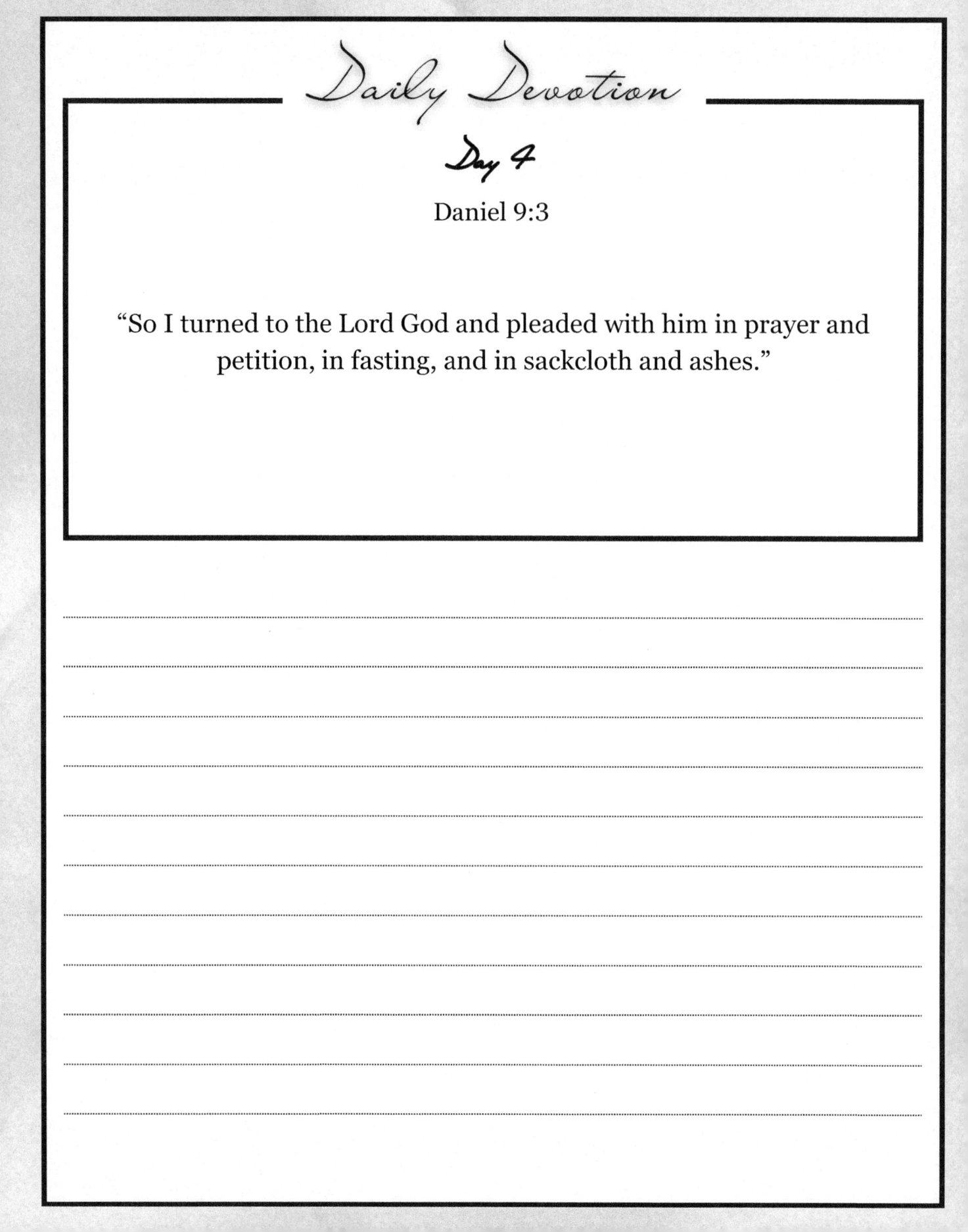

Day 4

Daniel 9:3

"So I turned to the Lord God and pleaded with him in prayer and petition, in fasting, and in sackcloth and ashes."

Daily Devotional

Date: M☐ T☐ W☐ T☐ F☐ S☐ S☐

Verse of The Day

_____
_____
_____

Key Words	Question

Reflection

_____
_____
_____

How Will I Apply This To My Life	My Prayerful Responses

Prayer

Date:_____

For Loved Ones _____

Self _____

Todays' Prayer Focus

_____
_____
_____
_____
_____
_____

Prayer Points

_____
_____
_____
_____
_____
_____
_____
_____
_____
_____
_____
_____

Prayer journal

Today's Date:

Today what is on my heart:

Today I am grateful for:

Prayer Request

Prayers Answered

Daily Devotion

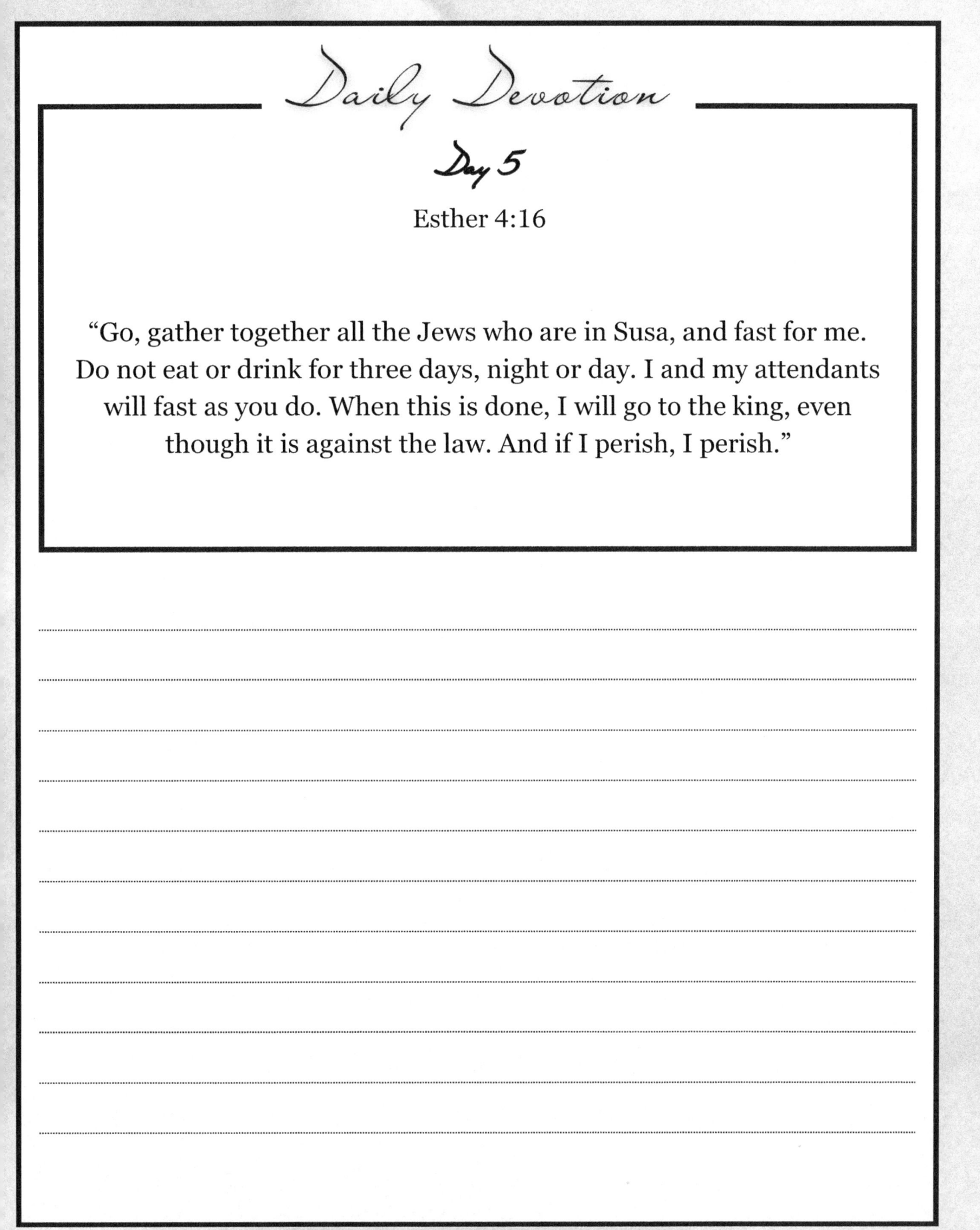

Day 5

Esther 4:16

"Go, gather together all the Jews who are in Susa, and fast for me. Do not eat or drink for three days, night or day. I and my attendants will fast as you do. When this is done, I will go to the king, even though it is against the law. And if I perish, I perish."

Daily Devotional

Date: M ☐ T ☐ W ☐ T ☐ F ☐ S ☐ S ☐

Verse of The Day

_____
_____
_____

Key Words	Question

Reflection

_____
_____
_____

How Will I Apply This To My Life	My Prayerful Responses

Prayer

For Loved Ones _____

Self _____

Todays' Prayer Focus

_____
_____
_____
_____
_____
_____

Date: _____

Prayer Points

_____
_____
_____
_____
_____
_____
_____
_____
_____
_____
_____

Prayer journal

Today's Date:

Today what is on my heart:

Today I am grateful for:

Prayer Request

Prayers Answered

Daily Devotion

Day 6

Nehemiah 1:4

"When I heard these things, I sat down and wept. For some days I mourned and fasted and prayed before the God of heaven."

Daily Devotional

Date:

M ☐ T ☐ W ☐ T ☐ F ☐ S ☐ S ☐

Verse of The Day

_____
_____
_____

Key Words	Question

Reflection

_____
_____
_____

How Will I Apply This To My Life	My Prayerful Responses

Prayer

Date: _____

For Loved Ones _____

Self _____

Todays' Prayer Focus

_____
_____
_____
_____
_____

Prayer Points

_____
_____
_____
_____
_____
_____
_____
_____
_____
_____
_____
_____

Prayer journal

Today's Date:

Today what is on my heart:

Today I am grateful for:

Prayer Request

Prayers Answered

Daily Devotion

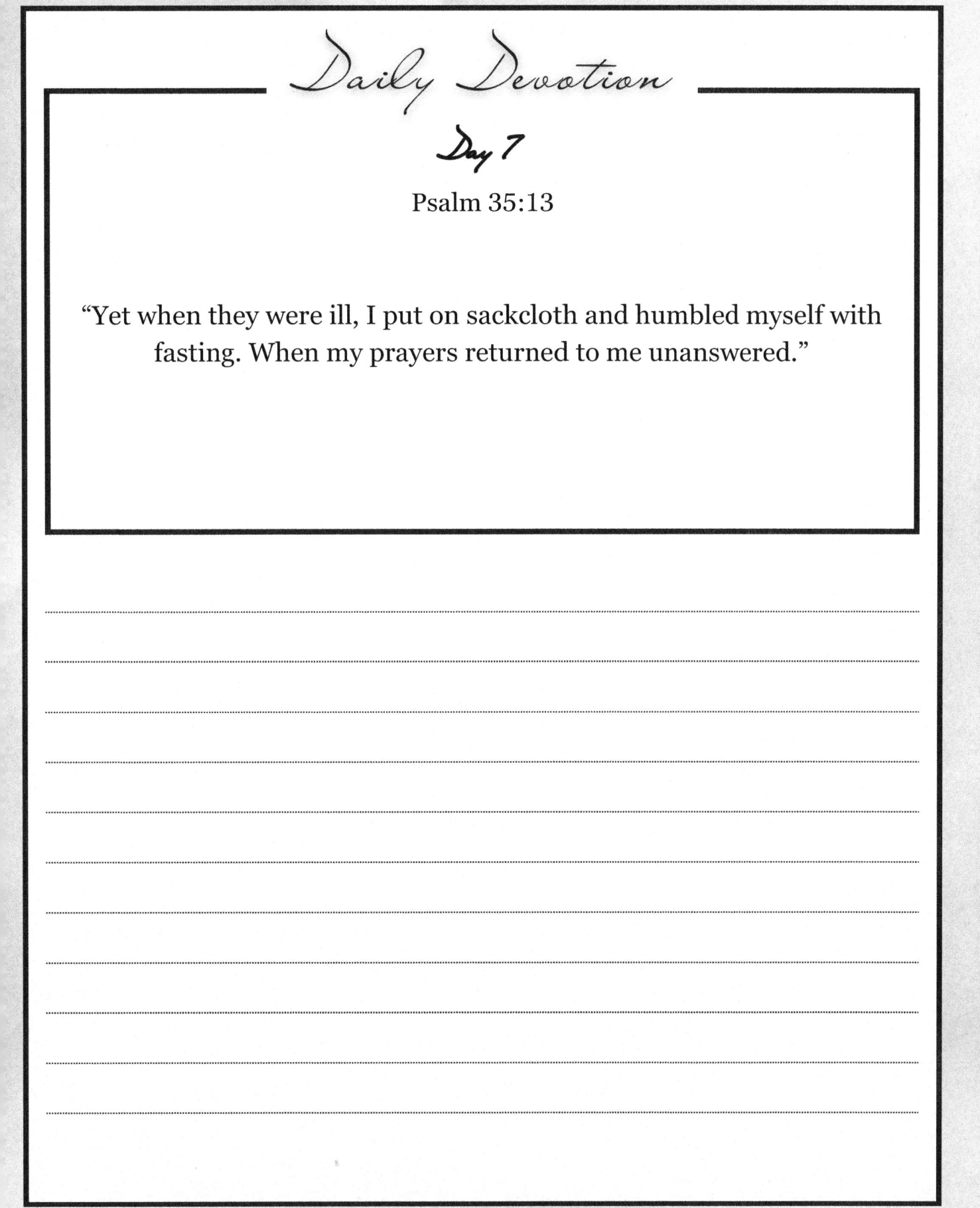

Day 7

Psalm 35:13

"Yet when they were ill, I put on sackcloth and humbled myself with fasting. When my prayers returned to me unanswered."

Daily Devotional

Date:

M ☐ T ☐ W ☐ T ☐ F ☐ S ☐ S ☐

Verse of The Day

_____

_____

_____

Key Words	Question

Reflection

_____

_____

_____

How Will I Apply This To My Life	My Prayerful Responses

Prayer

For Loved Ones _____

Self _____

Todays' Prayer Focus

_____
_____
_____
_____
_____
_____
_____

Date: _____

Prayer Points

_____
_____
_____
_____
_____
_____
_____
_____
_____
_____
_____
_____
_____

Prayer journal

Today's Date:

Today what is on my heart:

Today I am grateful for:

Prayer Request

Prayers Answered

Daily Devotion

Day 8

Matthew 6:16-18

"When you fast, do not look somber as the hypocrites do, for they disfigure their faces to show others they are fasting. Truly I tell you, they have their reward. But when you fast, put oil on your head and wash your face, so that it will not be obvious to others that you are fasting, but only to your Father, who is unseen; and your Father, who sees what is done in secret, will reward you."

Daily Devotional

Date:

M ☐ T ☐ W ☐ T ☐ F ☐ S ☐ S ☐

Verse of The Day

_____

_____

_____

Key Words	Question

Reflection

_____

_____

_____

How Will I Apply This To My Life	My Prayerful Responses

Prayer

Date: _____

For Loved Ones _____

Self _____

Todays' Prayer Focus

_____
_____
_____
_____
_____
_____

Prayer Points

_____
_____
_____
_____
_____
_____
_____
_____
_____
_____
_____
_____

Prayer journal

Today's Date:

Today what is on my heart:

Today I am grateful for:

Prayer Request

Prayers Answered

Daily Devotion

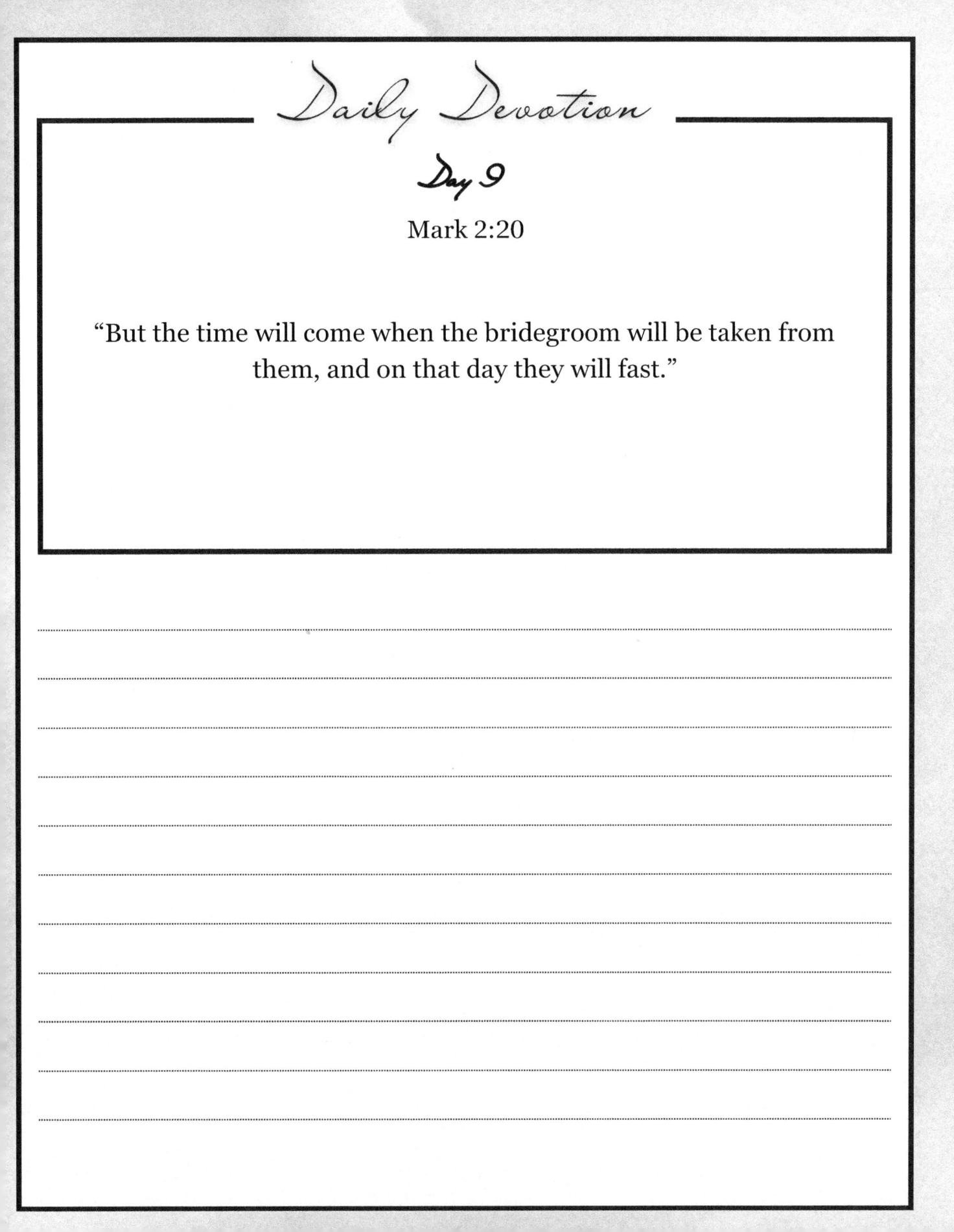

Day 9

Mark 2:20

"But the time will come when the bridegroom will be taken from them, and on that day they will fast."

Daily Devotional

Date:　　　　　　　M ☐ T ☐ W ☐ T ☐ F ☐ S ☐ S ☐

Verse of The Day

_____
_____
_____

Key Words	Question

Reflection

_____
_____
_____

How Will I Apply This To My Life	My Prayerful Responses

Prayer

For Loved Ones _____

Self _____

Todays' Prayer Focus

_____
_____
_____
_____
_____
_____

Date: _____

Prayer Points

_____
_____
_____
_____
_____
_____
_____
_____
_____
_____
_____
_____

Prayer journal

Today's Date:

Today what is on my heart:

Today I am grateful for:

Prayer Request

Prayers Answered

Daily Devotion

Day 10

Luke 4:2

"where for forty days he was tempted by the devil. He ate nothing during those days, and at the end of them, he was hungry."

Daily Devotional

Date:

M ☐ T ☐ W ☐ T ☐ F ☐ S ☐ S ☐

Verse of The Day

_____
_____
_____

Key Words	Question

Reflection

_____
_____
_____

How Will I Apply This To My Life	My Prayerful Responses

Date:_____

Prayer

For Loved Ones _____

Self _____

Todays' Prayer Focus

_____
_____
_____
_____
_____
_____

Prayer Points

_____
_____
_____
_____
_____
_____
_____
_____
_____
_____
_____
_____

Prayer journal

Today's Date:

Today what is on my heart:

Today I am grateful for:

Prayer Request

Prayers Answered

Daily Devotion

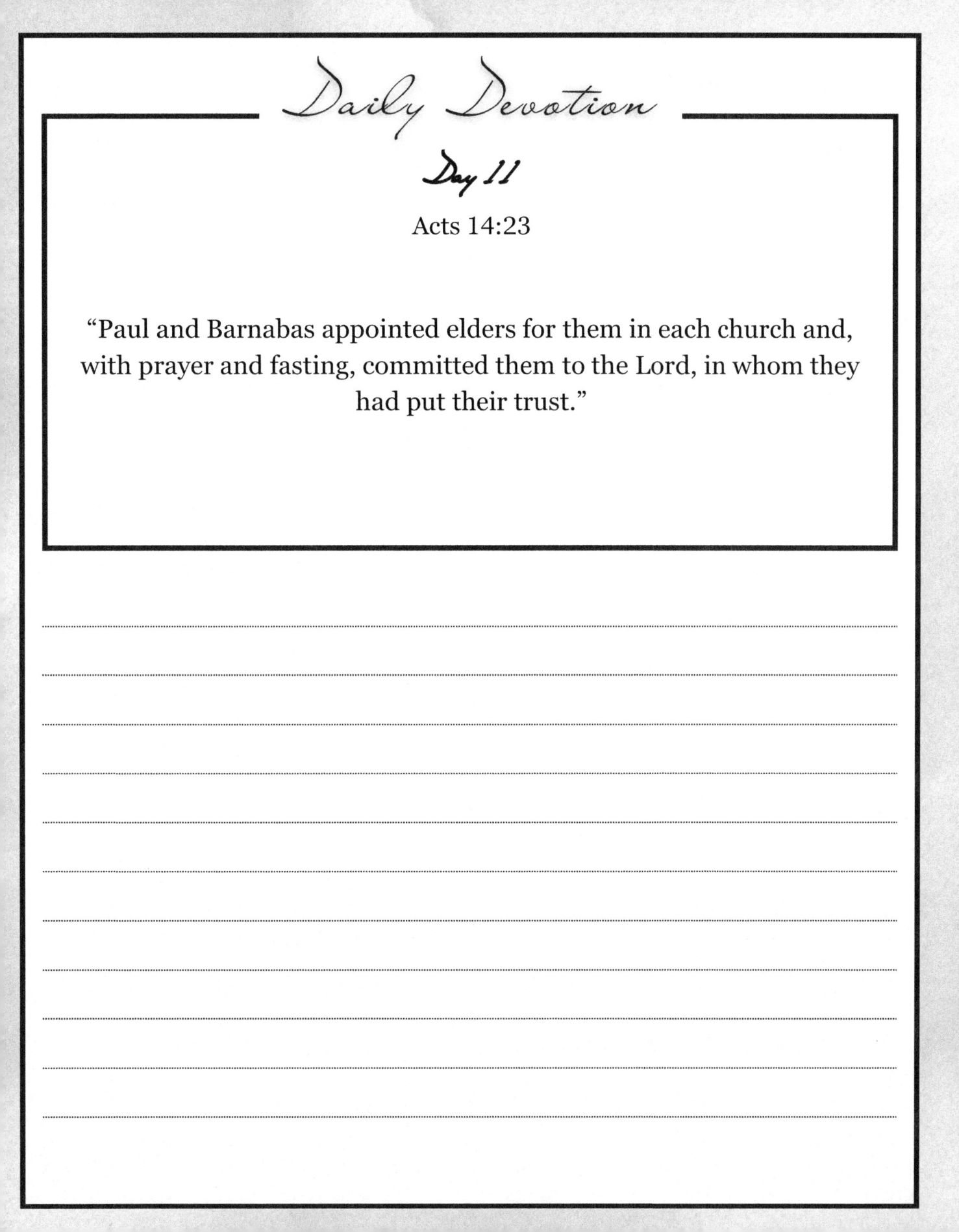

Day 11

Acts 14:23

"Paul and Barnabas appointed elders for them in each church and, with prayer and fasting, committed them to the Lord, in whom they had put their trust."

Daily Devotional

Date:　　　　　M ☐ T ☐ W ☐ T ☐ F ☐ S ☐ S ☐

Verse of The Day

_____

_____

_____

Key Words	Question

Reflection

_____

_____

_____

How Will I Apply This To My Life	My Prayerful Responses

Prayer

Date: _____

For Loved Ones _____

Self _____

Todays' Prayer Focus

_____
_____
_____
_____
_____
_____

Prayer Points

_____
_____
_____
_____
_____
_____
_____
_____
_____
_____
_____
_____

Prayer journal

Prayer

Date:_____

For Loved Ones _____

Self _____

Todays' Prayer Focus

_____
_____
_____
_____
_____
_____

Prayer Points

_____
_____
_____
_____
_____
_____
_____
_____
_____
_____
_____

Today's Date:

Today what is on my heart:

Today I am grateful for:

Prayer Request

Prayers Answered

Daily Devotion

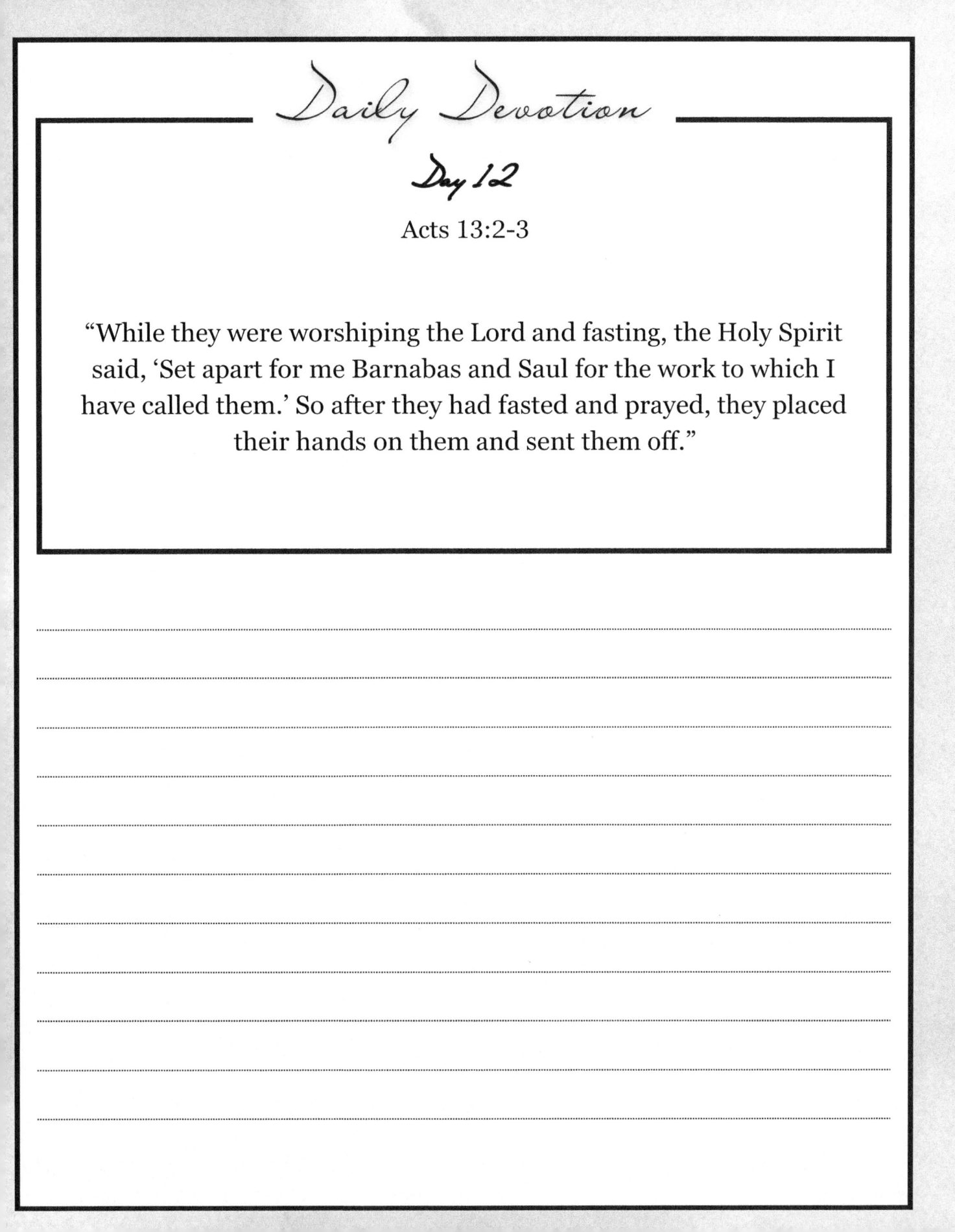

Day 12

Acts 13:2-3

"While they were worshiping the Lord and fasting, the Holy Spirit said, 'Set apart for me Barnabas and Saul for the work to which I have called them.' So after they had fasted and prayed, they placed their hands on them and sent them off."

Daily Devotional

Date: M ☐ T ☐ W ☐ T ☐ F ☐ S ☐ S ☐

Verse of The Day

_____

_____

_____

Key Words	Question

Reflection

_____

_____

_____

How Will I Apply This To My Life	My Prayerful Responses

Prayer

Date:_____

For Loved Ones _____

Self _____

Todays' Prayer Focus

_____
_____
_____
_____
_____
_____

Prayer Points

_____
_____
_____
_____
_____
_____
_____
_____
_____
_____
_____

Prayer journal

Today's Date:

Today what is on my heart:

Today I am grateful for:

Prayer Request

Prayers Answered

Daily Devotion

Day 13

Isaiah 58:3-5

"'Why have we fasted,' they say, 'and you have not seen it? Why have we humbled ourselves, and you have not noticed?' Yet on the day of your fasting, you do as you please and exploit all your workers. Your fasting ends in quarreling and strife, and in striking each other with wicked fists. You cannot fast as you do today and expect your voice to be heard on high."

Daily Devotional

Date:

M ☐ T ☐ W ☐ T ☐ F ☐ S ☐ S ☐

Verse of The Day

_____
_____
_____

Key Words	Question

Reflection

_____
_____
_____

How Will I Apply This To My Life	My Prayerful Responses

Prayer

Date: _____

For Loved Ones _____

Self _____

Todays' Prayer Focus

_____
_____
_____
_____
_____

Prayer Points

_____
_____
_____
_____
_____
_____
_____
_____
_____
_____

Prayer journal

Today's Date:

Today what is on my heart:

Today I am grateful for:

Prayer Request

Prayers Answered

Daily Devotion

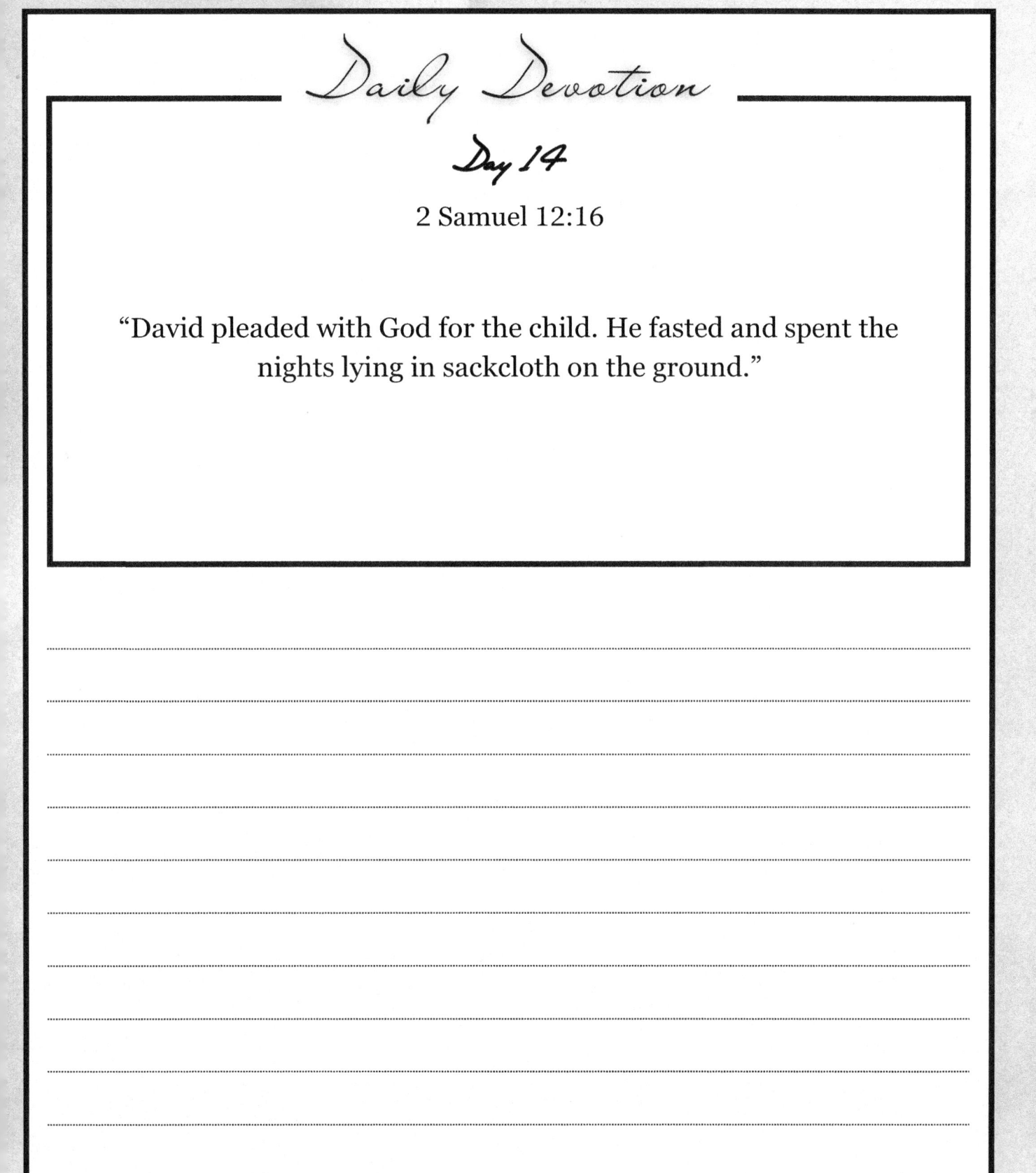

Day 14

2 Samuel 12:16

"David pleaded with God for the child. He fasted and spent the nights lying in sackcloth on the ground."

Daily Devotional

Date: M O T O W O T O F O S O S O

Verse of The Day

_____
_____
_____

Key Words	Question

Reflection

_____
_____
_____

How Will I Apply This To My Life	My Prayerful Responses

Prayer

For Loved Ones _____

Self _____

Todays' Prayer Focus

Date:_____

_____
_____
_____
_____
_____
_____

Prayer Points

_____
_____
_____
_____
_____
_____
_____
_____
_____
_____
_____
_____
_____

Prayer journal

Prayer

Date: _____

For Loved Ones _____

Self _____

Todays' Prayer Focus

_____
_____
_____
_____
_____
_____

Prayer Points

_____
_____
_____
_____
_____
_____
_____
_____
_____
_____

Today's Date:

Today what is on my heart:

Today I am grateful for:

Prayer Request

Prayers Answered

Daily Devotion

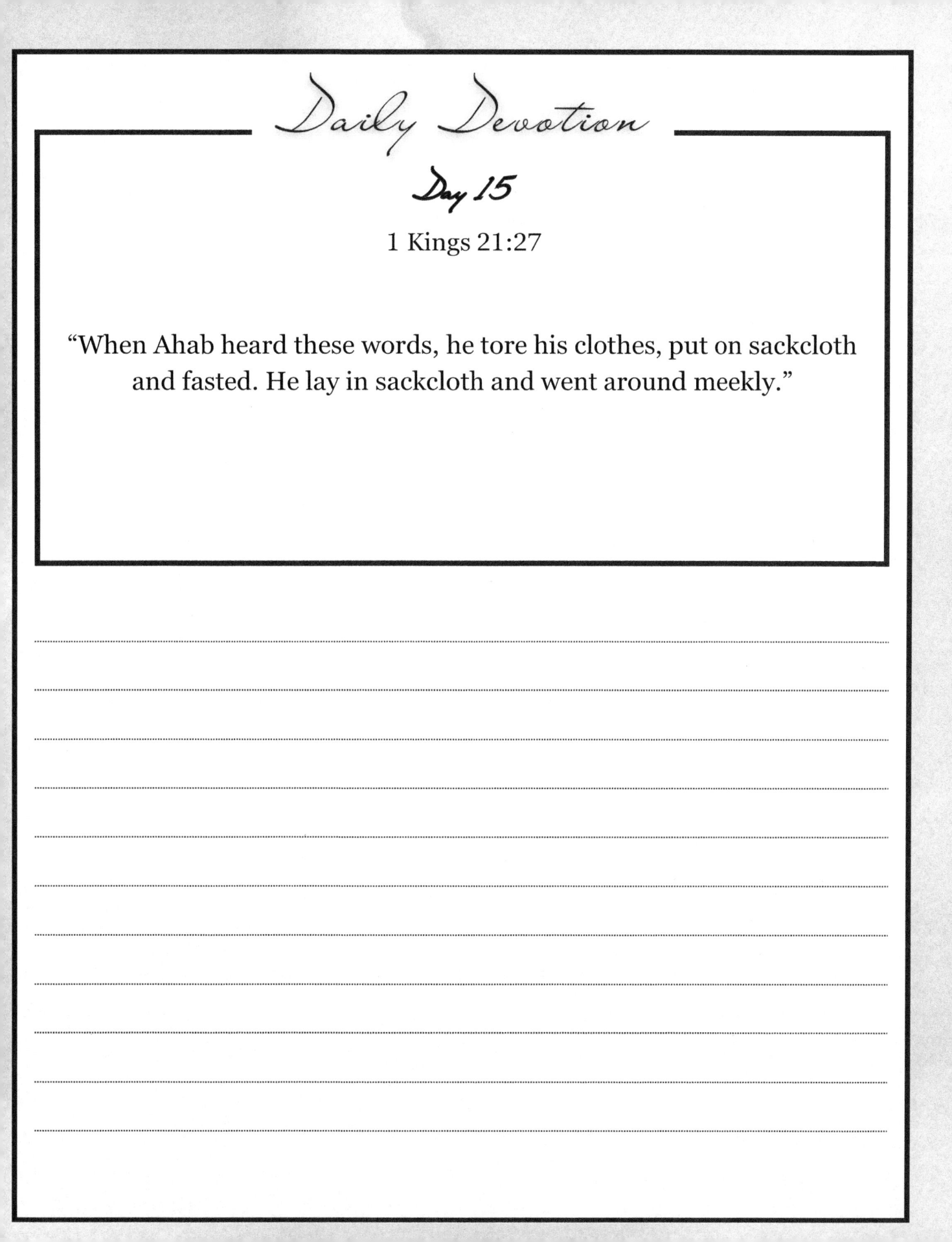

Day 15

1 Kings 21:27

"When Ahab heard these words, he tore his clothes, put on sackcloth and fasted. He lay in sackcloth and went around meekly."

Daily Devotional

Date:

M ☐ T ☐ W ☐ T ☐ F ☐ S ☐ S ☐

Verse of The Day

_____

_____

_____

Key Words	Question

Reflection

_____

_____

_____

How Will I Apply This To My Life	My Prayerful Responses

Prayer

Date: _____

For Loved Ones _____

Self _____

Todays' Prayer Focus

_____
_____
_____
_____
_____
_____

Prayer Points

_____
_____
_____
_____
_____
_____
_____
_____
_____
_____
_____

Prayer journal

Today's Date:

Today what is on my heart:

Today I am grateful for:

Prayer Request

Prayers Answered

Daily Devotion

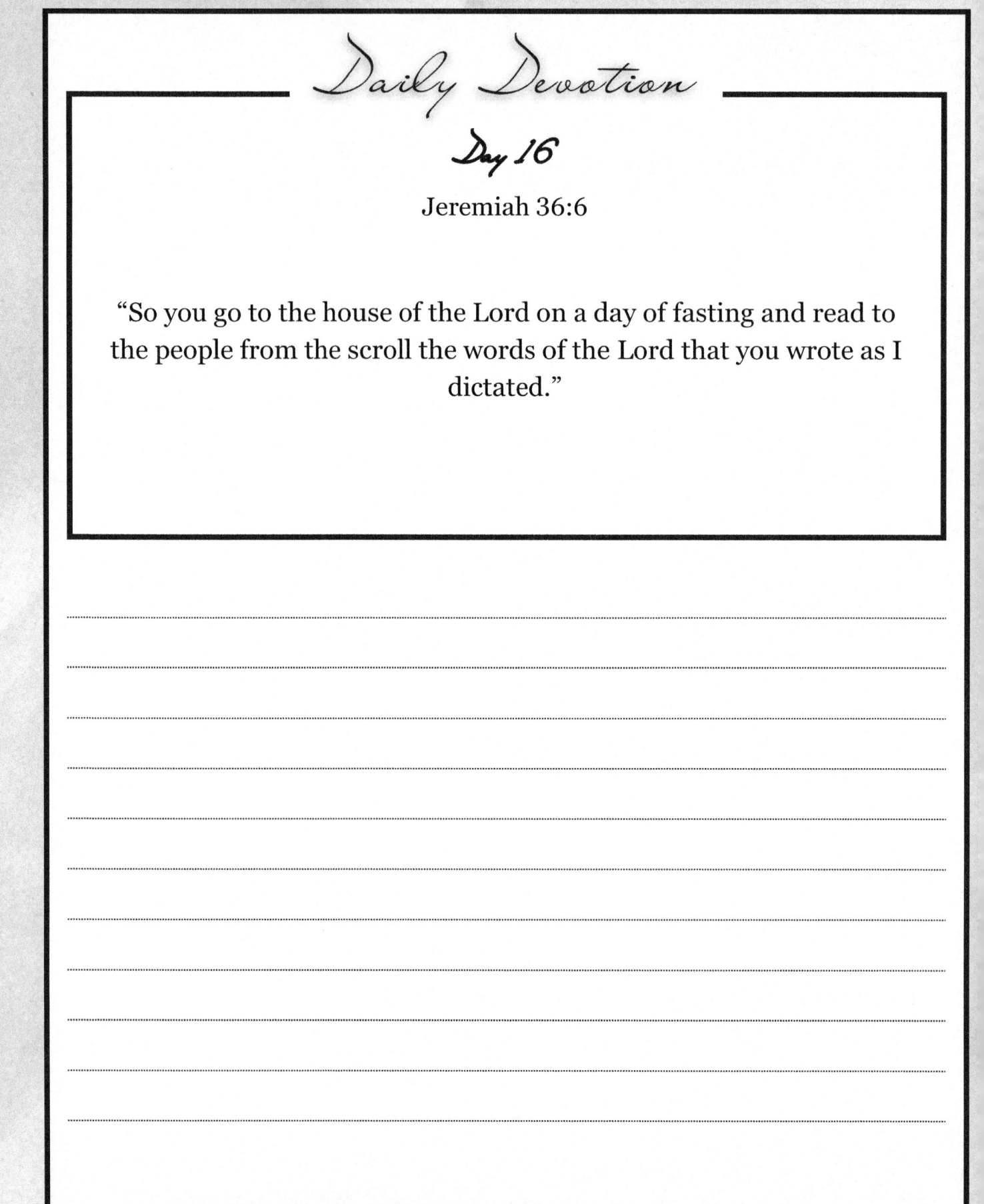

Day 16

Jeremiah 36:6

"So you go to the house of the Lord on a day of fasting and read to the people from the scroll the words of the Lord that you wrote as I dictated."

Daily Devotional

Date: M☐ T☐ W☐ T☐ F☐ S☐ S☐

Verse of The Day

_____
_____
_____

Key Words	Question

Reflection

_____
_____
_____

How Will I Apply This To My Life	My Prayerful Responses

Prayer

Date: _____

For Loved Ones _____

Self _____

Todays' Prayer Focus

_____
_____
_____
_____
_____
_____

Prayer Points

_____
_____
_____
_____
_____
_____
_____
_____
_____
_____
_____
_____

Prayer journal

Today's Date:

Today what is on my heart:

Today I am grateful for:

Prayer Request

Prayers Answered

Daily Devotion

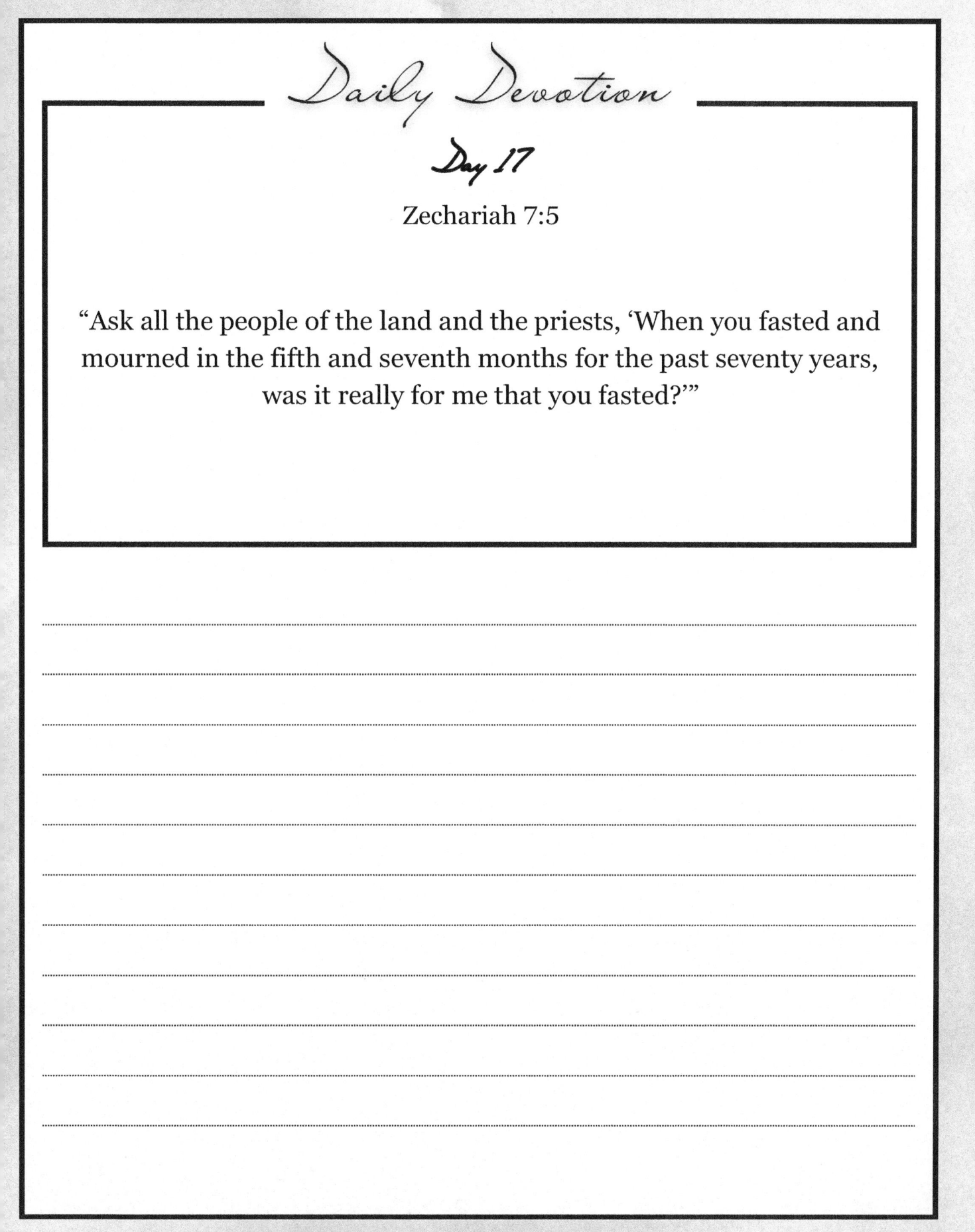

Day 17

Zechariah 7:5

"Ask all the people of the land and the priests, 'When you fasted and mourned in the fifth and seventh months for the past seventy years, was it really for me that you fasted?'"

Daily Devotional

Date:

M ☐ T ☐ W ☐ T ☐ F ☐ S ☐ S ☐

Verse of The Day

_____
_____
_____

Key Words	Question

Reflection

_____
_____
_____

How Will I Apply This To My Life	My Prayerful Responses

Prayer

For Loved Ones _____

Self _____

Todays' Prayer Focus

_____
_____
_____
_____
_____
_____

Prayer Points

_____
_____
_____
_____
_____
_____
_____
_____
_____
_____
_____
_____

Date:_____

Prayer journal

Today's Date:

Today what is on my heart:

Today I am grateful for:

Prayer Request

Prayers Answered

Daily Devotion

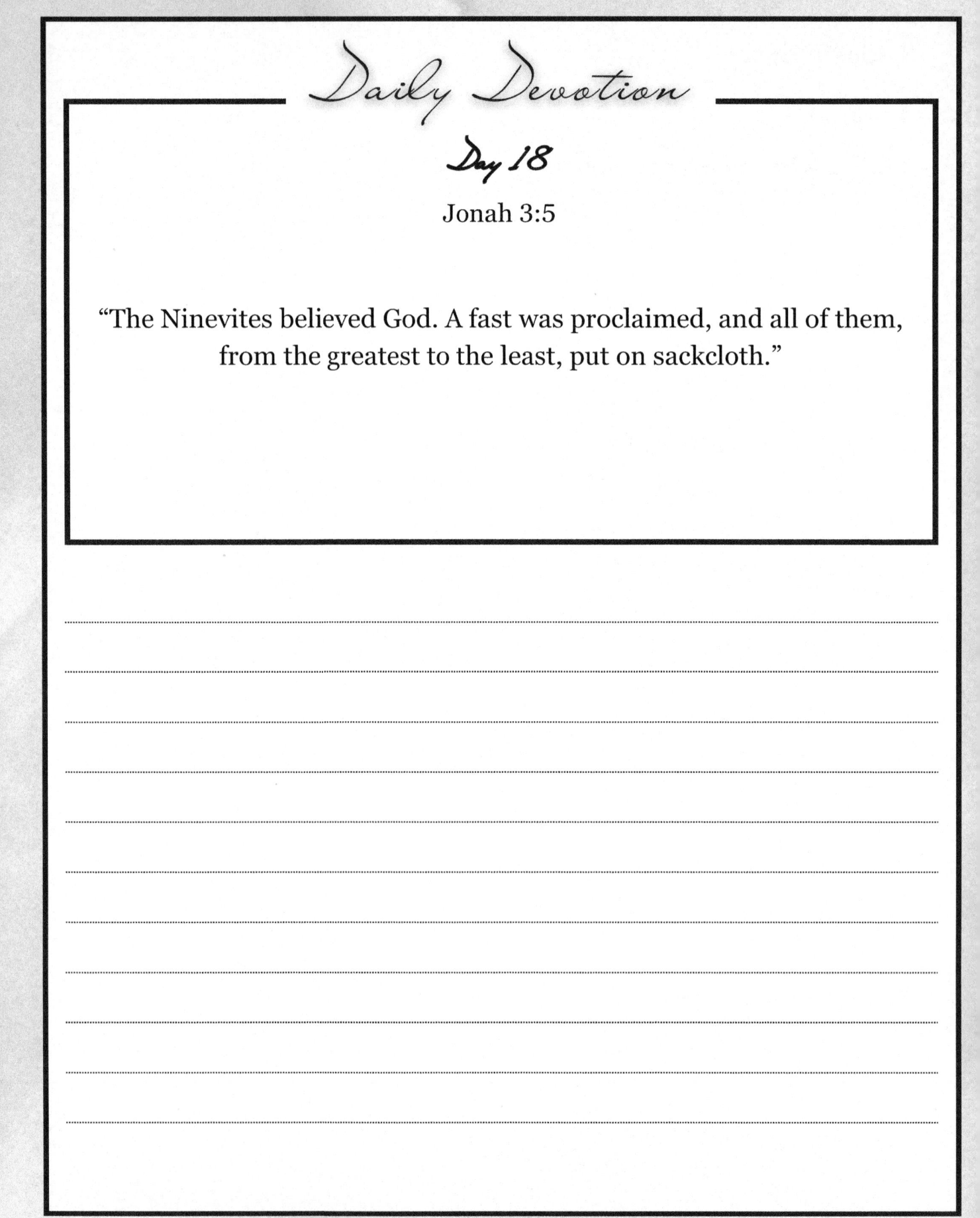

Day 18

Jonah 3:5

"The Ninevites believed God. A fast was proclaimed, and all of them, from the greatest to the least, put on sackcloth."

Daily Devotional

Date: M ☐ T ☐ W ☐ T ☐ F ☐ S ☐ S ☐

Verse of The Day

_____
_____
_____

Key Words	Question

Reflection

_____
_____
_____

How Will I Apply This To My Life	My Prayerful Responses

Prayer

Date: _____

For Loved Ones _____

Self _____

Todays' Prayer Focus

_____
_____
_____
_____
_____

Prayer Points

_____
_____
_____
_____
_____
_____
_____
_____
_____
_____
_____
_____

Prayer journal

Today's Date:

Today what is on my heart:

Today I am grateful for:

Prayer Request

Prayers Answered

Daily Devotion

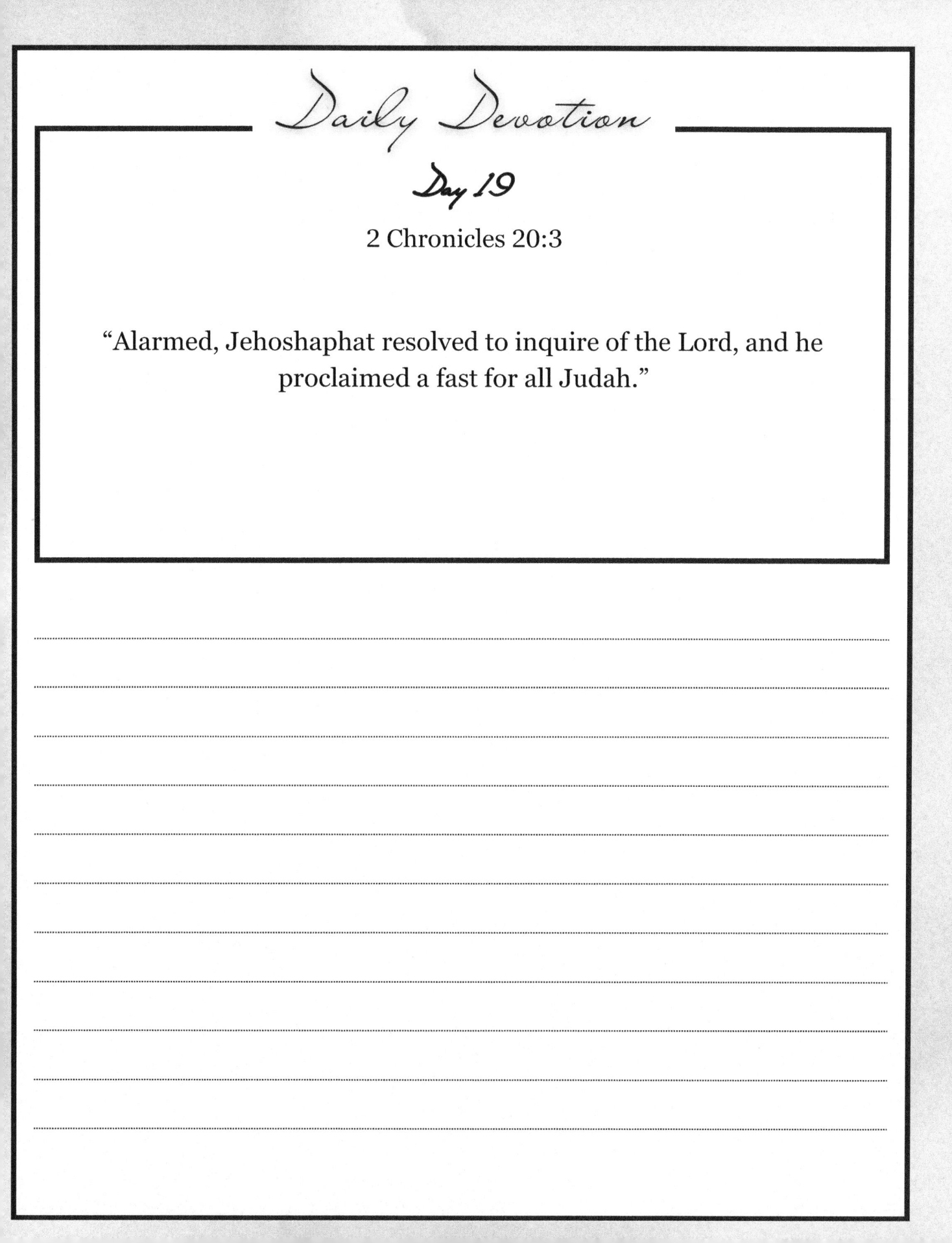

Day 19

2 Chronicles 20:3

"Alarmed, Jehoshaphat resolved to inquire of the Lord, and he proclaimed a fast for all Judah."

Daily Devotional

Date:

M ☐ T ☐ W ☐ T ☐ F ☐ S ☐ S ☐

Verse of The Day

_____
_____
_____

Key Words	Question

Reflection

_____
_____
_____

How Will I Apply This To My Life	My Prayerful Responses

Prayer

For Loved Ones _____

Self _____

Todays' Prayer Focus

_____
_____
_____
_____
_____
_____

Date: _____

Prayer Points

_____
_____
_____
_____
_____
_____
_____
_____
_____

Prayer journal

Today's Date:

Today what is on my heart:

Today I am grateful for:

Prayer Request

Prayers Answered

Daily Devotion

Day 20

Matthew 9:14-15

"Then John's disciples came and asked him, 'How is it that we and the Pharisees fast often, but your disciples do not fast?' Jesus answered, 'How can the guests of the bridegroom mourn while he is with them? The time will come when the bridegroom will be taken from them; then they will fast.'"

Daily Devotional

Date:

M☐ T☐ W☐ T☐ F☐ S☐ S☐

Verse of The Day

_____
_____
_____

Key Words	Question

Reflection

_____
_____
_____

How Will I Apply This To My Life	My Prayerful Responses

Prayer

Date:_____

For Loved Ones _____

Self _____

Todays' Prayer Focus

_____
_____
_____
_____
_____

Prayer Points

_____
_____
_____
_____
_____
_____
_____
_____
_____
_____
_____

Prayer journal

Today's Date:

Today what is on my heart:

Today I am grateful for:

Prayer Request

Prayers Answered

Daily Devotion

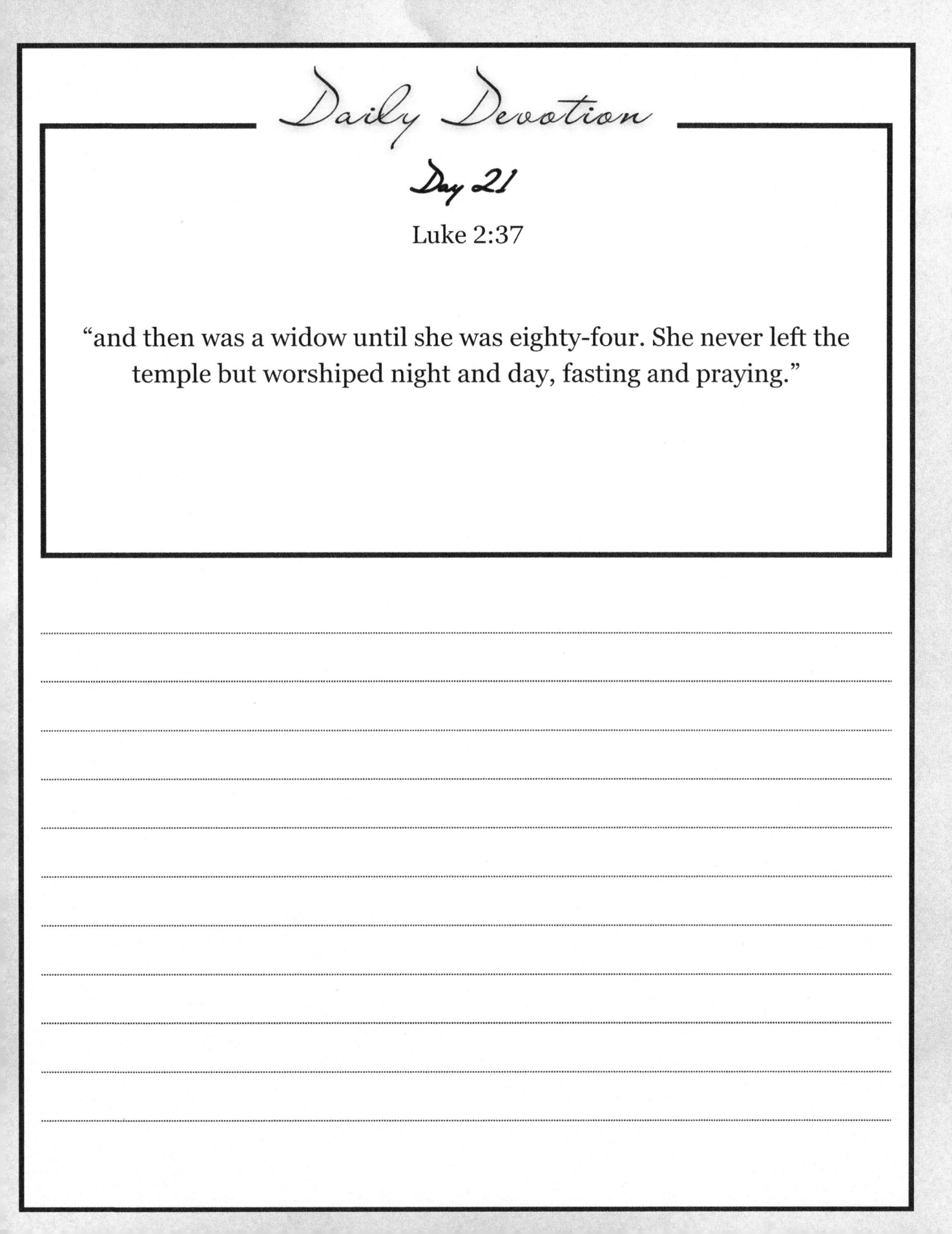

Day 21

Luke 2:37

"and then was a widow until she was eighty-four. She never left the temple but worshiped night and day, fasting and praying."

Daily Devotional

Date:　　　　　　　　M ☐ T ☐ W ☐ T ☐ F ☐ S ☐ S ☐

Verse of The Day

_____
_____
_____

Key Words	Question

Reflection

_____
_____
_____

How Will I Apply This To My Life	My Prayerful Responses

Prayer

Date:_____

For Loved Ones _____

Self _____

Todays' Prayer Focus

_____
_____
_____
_____
_____
_____

Prayer Points

_____
_____
_____
_____
_____
_____
_____
_____
_____
_____
_____
_____

Prayer journal

Today's Date:

Today what is on my heart:

Today I am grateful for:

Prayer Request

Prayers Answered

Daily Devotion

Day 22

Acts 13:3

"So after they had fasted and prayed, they placed their hands on them and sent them off."

Daily Devotional

Date:

M ☐ T ☐ W ☐ T ☐ F ☐ S ☐ S ☐

Verse of The Day

_____
_____
_____

Key Words	Question

Reflection

_____
_____
_____

How Will I Apply This To My Life	My Prayerful Responses

Prayer

Date: _____

For Loved Ones _____

Self _____

Todays' Prayer Focus

_____

_____

_____

_____

_____

_____

Prayer Points

_____

_____

_____

_____

_____

_____

_____

_____

_____

_____

_____

_____

Prayer journal

Today's Date:

Today what is on my heart:

Today I am grateful for:

Prayer Request

Prayers Answered

Daily Devotion

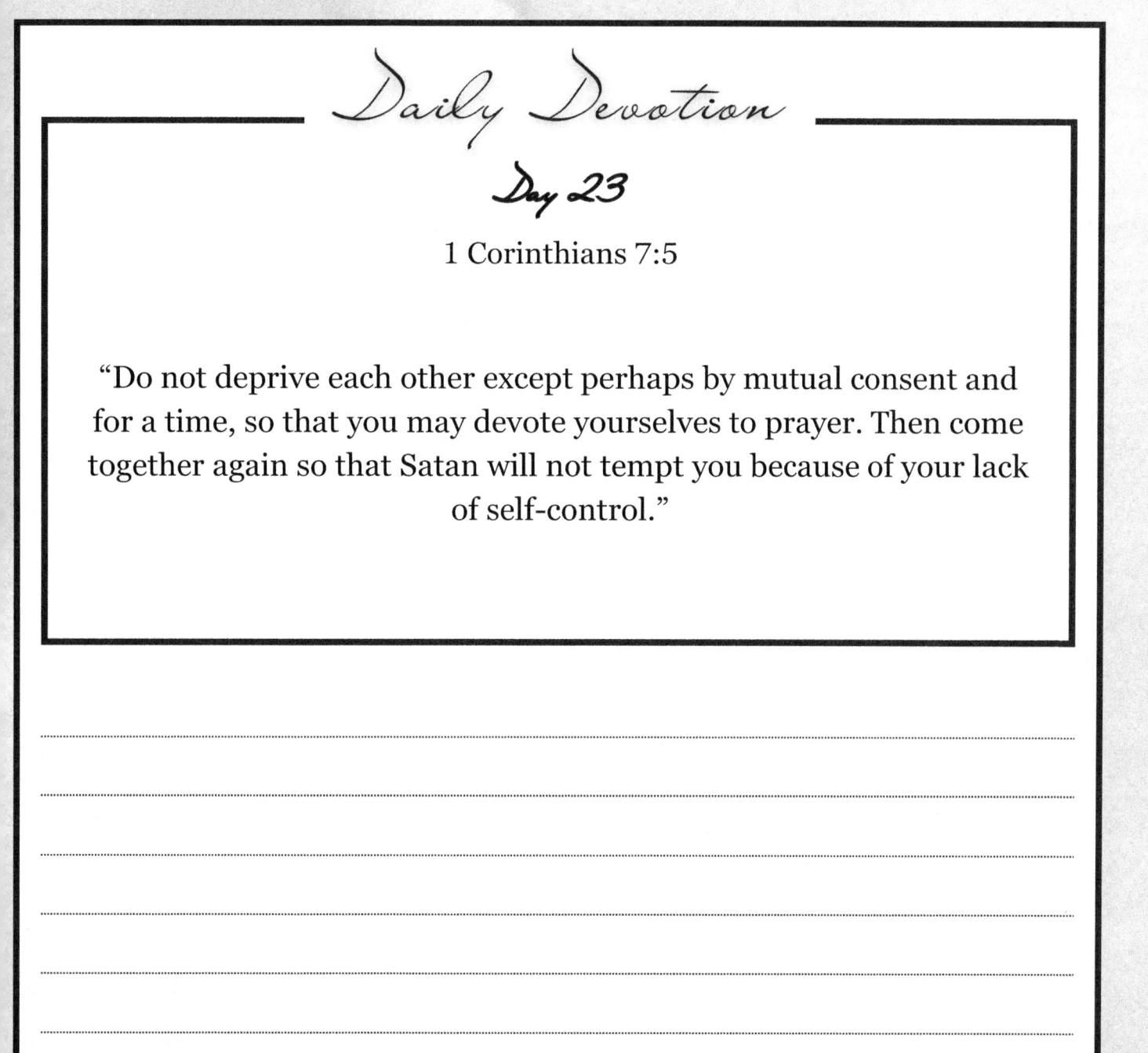

Day 23

1 Corinthians 7:5

"Do not deprive each other except perhaps by mutual consent and for a time, so that you may devote yourselves to prayer. Then come together again so that Satan will not tempt you because of your lack of self-control."

Daily Devotional

Date:

MOTOWO TO FOSOSO

Verse of The Day

_____
_____
_____

Key Words	Question

Reflection

_____
_____
_____

How Will I Apply This To My Life	My Prayerful Responses

Prayer

Date: _____

For Loved Ones _____

Self _____

Todays' Prayer Focus

_____
_____
_____
_____
_____
_____

Prayer Points

_____
_____
_____
_____
_____
_____
_____
_____
_____
_____
_____

Prayer journal

Today's Date:

Today what is on my heart:

Today I am grateful for:

Prayer Request

Prayers Answered

Daily Devotion

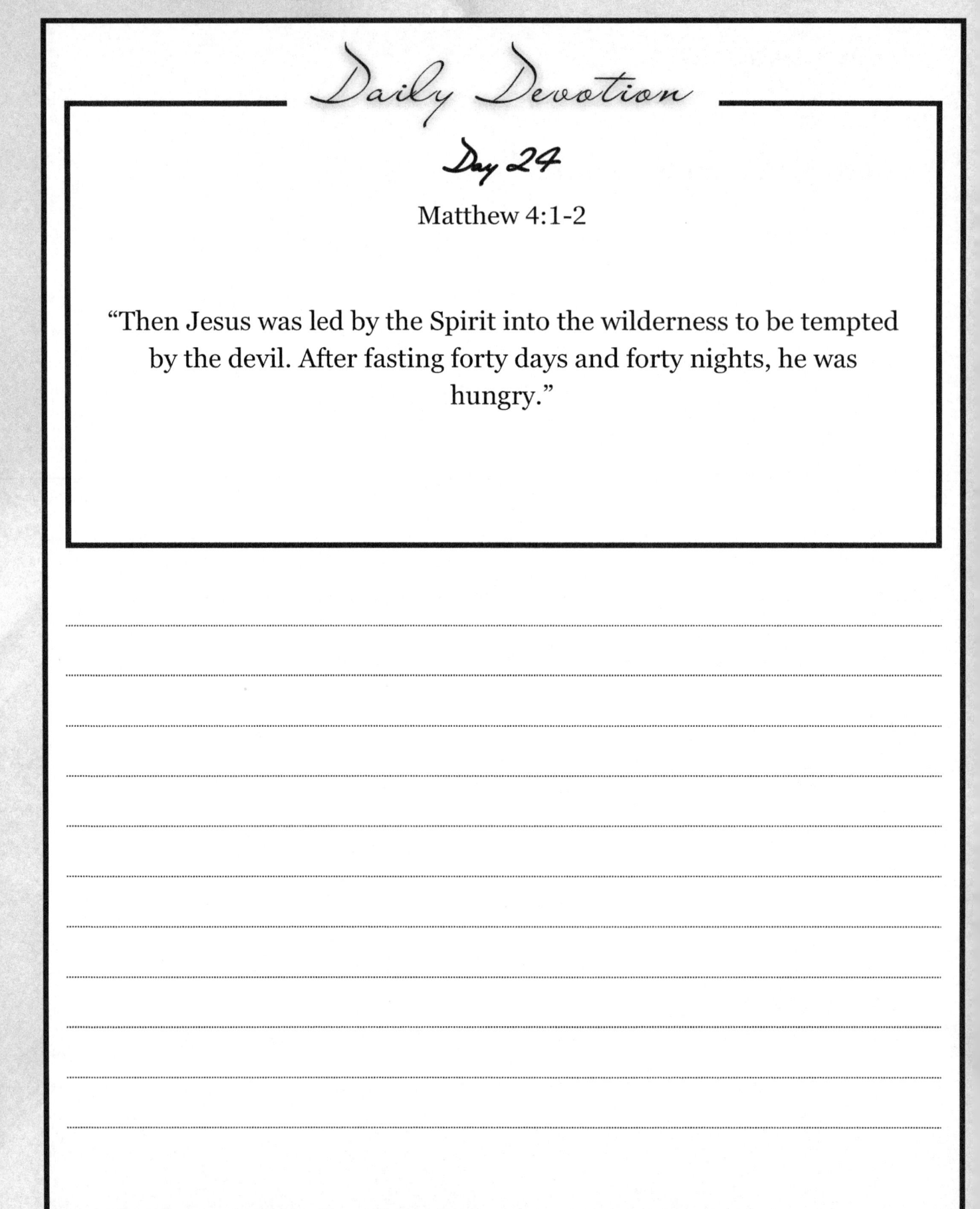

Day 24

Matthew 4:1-2

"Then Jesus was led by the Spirit into the wilderness to be tempted by the devil. After fasting forty days and forty nights, he was hungry."

Daily Devotional

Date:

M☐ T☐ W☐ T☐ F☐ S☐ S☐

Verse of The Day

_____

_____

_____

Key Words	Question

Reflection

_____

_____

_____

How Will I Apply This To My Life	My Prayerful Responses

Date:_____

Prayer

For Loved Ones _____

Self _____

Todays' Prayer Focus

_____
_____
_____
_____
_____
_____

Prayer Points

_____
_____
_____
_____
_____
_____
_____
_____
_____
_____
_____

Prayer journal

Today's Date:

Today what is on my heart:

Today I am grateful for:

Prayer Request

Prayers Answered

Daily Devotion

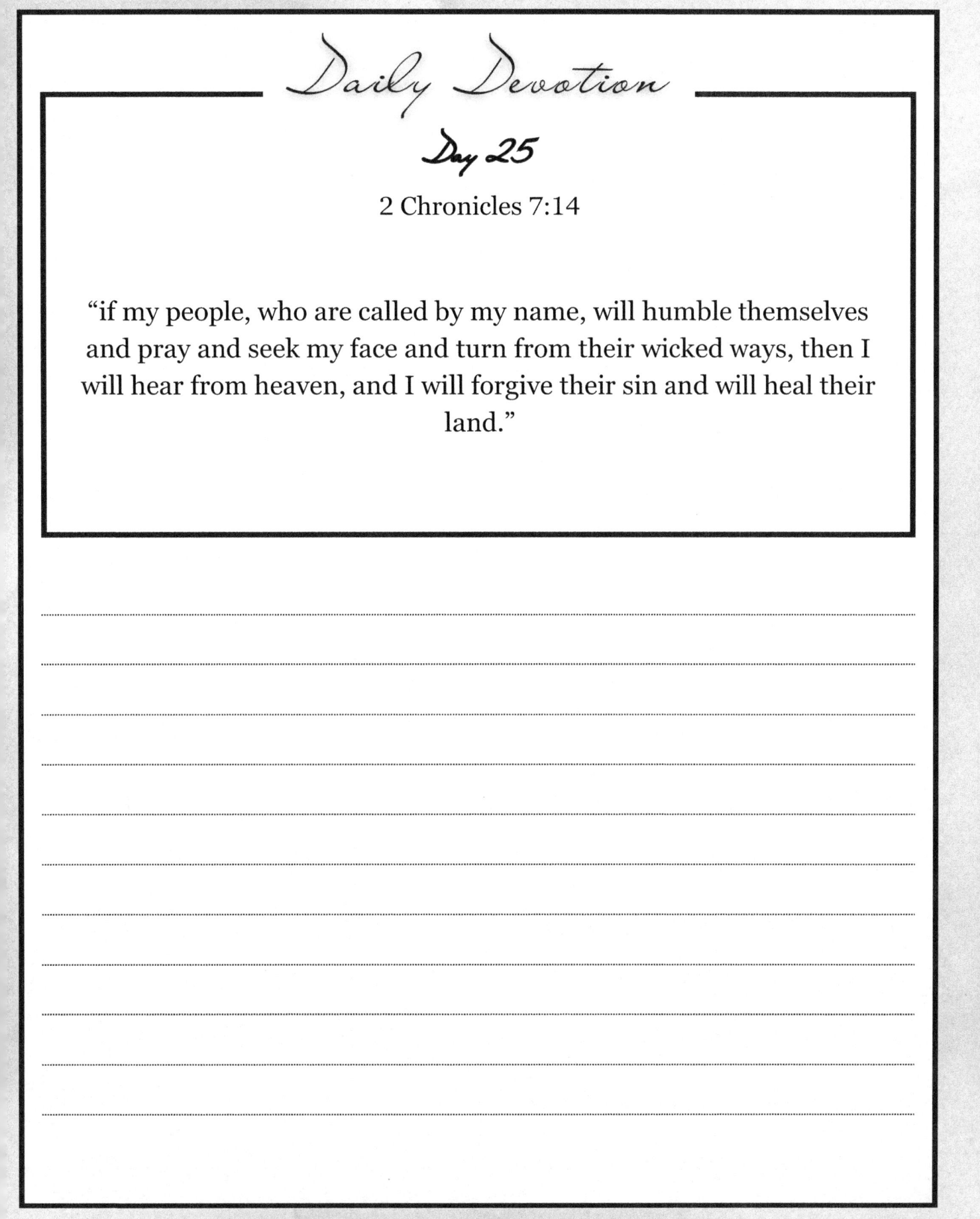

Day 25

2 Chronicles 7:14

"if my people, who are called by my name, will humble themselves and pray and seek my face and turn from their wicked ways, then I will hear from heaven, and I will forgive their sin and will heal their land."

Daily Devotional

Date: MOTOWO TO FOSOSO

Verse of The Day

_____

_____

_____

Key Words	Question

Reflection

_____

_____

_____

How Will I Apply This To My Life	My Prayerful Responses

Prayer

Date: _____

For Loved Ones _____

Self _____

Todays' Prayer Focus

_____
_____
_____
_____
_____
_____

Prayer Points

_____
_____
_____
_____
_____
_____
_____
_____
_____
_____
_____
_____

Prayer journal

Today's Date:

Today what is on my heart:

Today I am grateful for:

Prayer Request

Prayers Answered

Daily Devotion

Day 26

Joel 1:14

"Declare a holy fast; call a sacred assembly. Summon the elders and all who live in the land to the house of the Lord your God, and cry out to the Lord."

Daily Devotional

Date:

MOTOWO TO FOSOSO

Verse of The Day

_____
_____
_____

Key Words	Question

Reflection

_____
_____
_____

How Will I Apply This To My Life	My Prayerful Responses

Prayer

Date: _____

For Loved Ones _____

Self _____

Todays' Prayer Focus

_____
_____
_____
_____
_____
_____

Prayer Points

_____
_____
_____
_____
_____
_____
_____
_____
_____
_____
_____
_____

Prayer journal

Today's Date:

Today what is on my heart:

Today I am grateful for:

Prayer Request

Prayers Answered

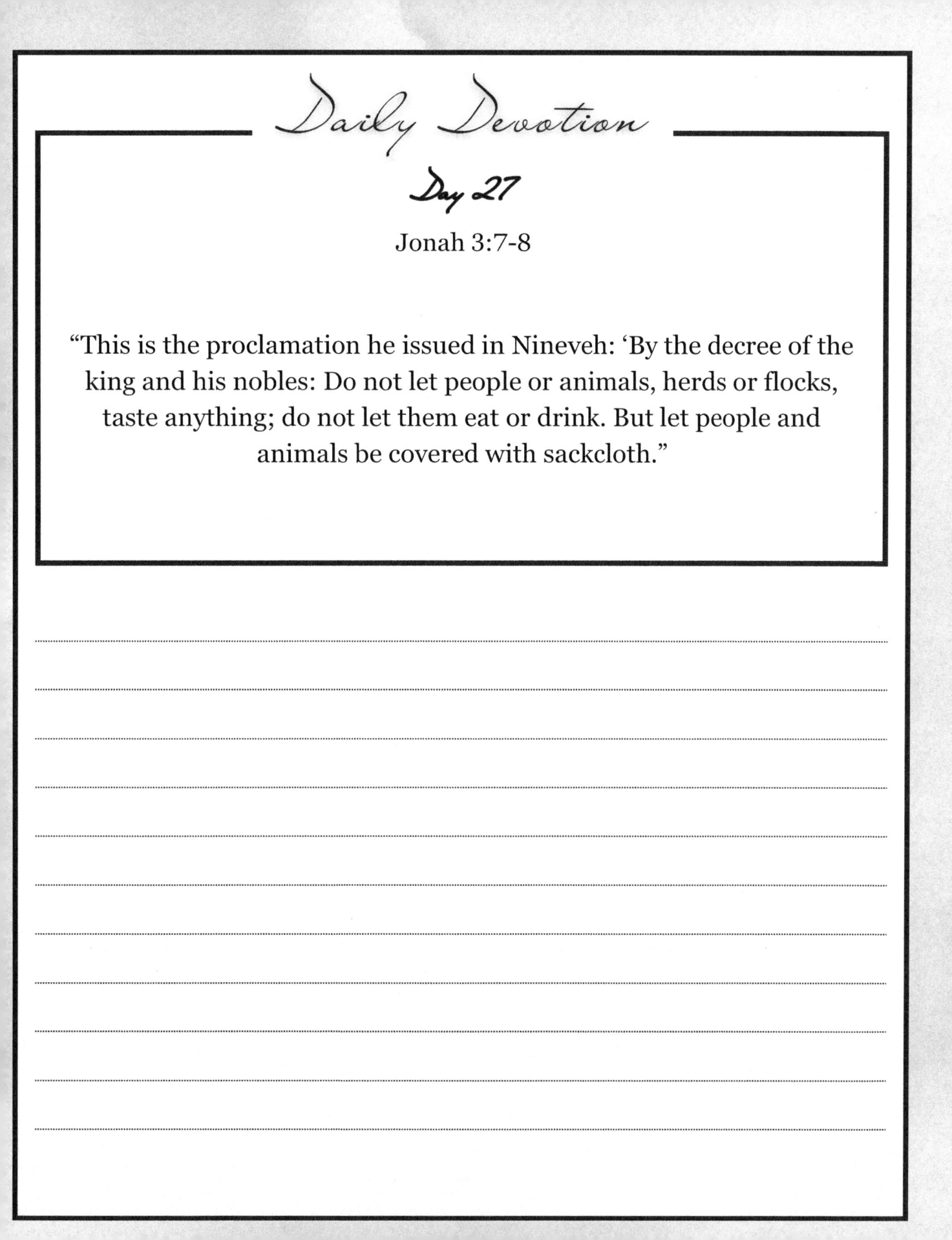

Daily Devotion

Day 27

Jonah 3:7-8

"This is the proclamation he issued in Nineveh: 'By the decree of the king and his nobles: Do not let people or animals, herds or flocks, taste anything; do not let them eat or drink. But let people and animals be covered with sackcloth."

Daily Devotional

Date:

M ☐ T ☐ W ☐ T ☐ F ☐ S ☐ S ☐

Verse of The Day

_____

_____

_____

Key Words	Question

Reflection

_____

_____

_____

How Will I Apply This To My Life	My Prayerful Responses

Prayer

Date: _____

For Loved Ones _____

Self _____

Todays' Prayer Focus

_____
_____
_____
_____
_____
_____

Prayer Points

_____
_____
_____
_____
_____
_____
_____
_____
_____
_____

Prayer journal

Today's Date:

Today what is on my heart:

Today I am grateful for:

Prayer Request

Prayers Answered

Daily Devotion

Day 28

Nehemiah 9:1-3

"On the twenty-fourth day of the same month, the Israelites gathered together, fasting and wearing sackcloth and putting dust on their heads. Those of Israelite descent had separated themselves from all foreigners. They stood in their places and confessed their sins and the sins of their ancestors."

Daily Devotional

Date:

M ☐ T ☐ W ☐ T ☐ F ☐ S ☐ S ☐

Verse of The Day

_____
_____
_____

Key Words	Question

Reflection

_____
_____
_____

How Will I Apply This To My Life	My Prayerful Responses

Prayer

Date: _____

For Loved Ones _____

Self _____

Todays' Prayer Focus

_____
_____
_____
_____
_____
_____

Prayer Points

_____
_____
_____
_____
_____
_____
_____
_____
_____
_____
_____

Prayer journal

Today's Date:

Today what is on my heart:

Today I am grateful for:

Prayer Request

Prayers Answered

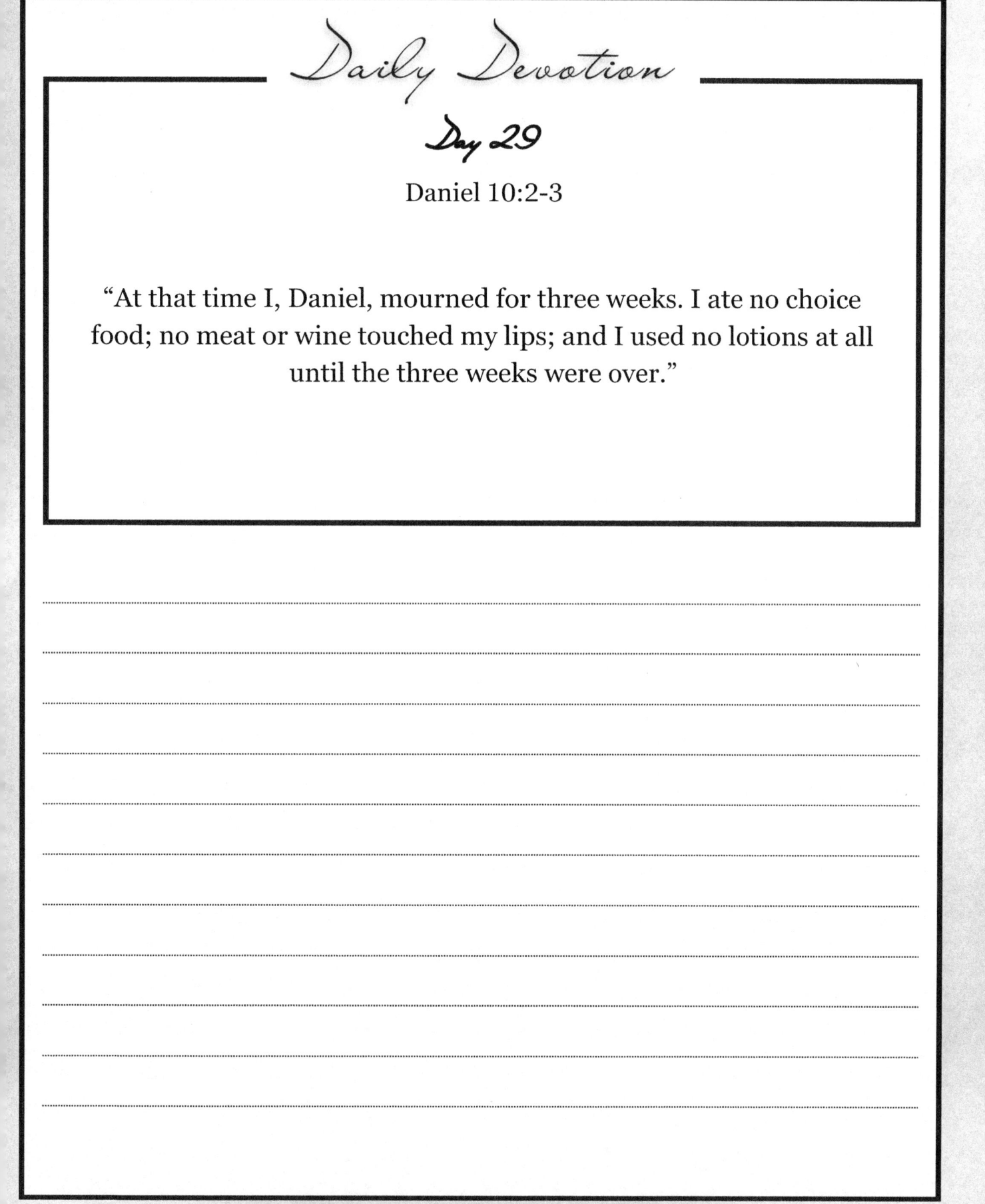

Daily Devotion

Day 29

Daniel 10:2-3

"At that time I, Daniel, mourned for three weeks. I ate no choice food; no meat or wine touched my lips; and I used no lotions at all until the three weeks were over."

Daily Devotional

Date:

M ☐ T ☐ W ☐ T ☐ F ☐ S ☐ S ☐

Verse of The Day

_____

_____

_____

Key Words	Question

Reflection

_____

_____

_____

How Will I Apply This To My Life	My Prayerful Responses

Prayer

For Loved Ones _____

Self _____

Todays' Prayer Focus

_____
_____
_____
_____
_____
_____

Date: _____

Prayer Points

_____
_____
_____
_____
_____
_____
_____
_____
_____
_____
_____
_____

Prayer journal

Today's Date:

Today what is on my heart:

Today I am grateful for:

Prayer Request

Prayers Answered

Daily Devotion

Day 30

Psalm 69:10

"When I weep and fast, I must endure scorn; when I put on sackcloth, people make sport of me."

Daily Devotional

Date: M ☐ T ☐ W ☐ T ☐ F ☐ S ☐ S ☐

Verse of The Day

_____

_____

_____

Key Words	Question

Reflection

_____

_____

_____

How Will I Apply This To My Life	My Prayerful Responses

Prayer

Date: _____

For Loved Ones _____

Self _____

Todays' Prayer Focus

_____
_____
_____
_____
_____
_____

Prayer Points

_____
_____
_____
_____
_____
_____
_____
_____
_____
_____
_____
_____

Prayer journal

Today's Date:

Today what is on my heart:

Today I am grateful for:

Prayer Request

Prayers Answered

Prayer List

Date	Individual	Prayer Needed

Prayer Request

Date	Requests	Answers

Printed in Dunstable, United Kingdom